I HUNT

TERRY LEE MCCLAIN

authorHOUSE®

AuthorHouse™
1663 Liberty Drive
Bloomington, IN 47403
www.authorhouse.com
Phone: 1-800-839-8640

Published by AuthorHouse 2/27/2013

ISBN: 978-1-4817-1968-1 (sc)
ISBN: 978-1-4817-1969-8 (e)

Library of Congress Control Number: 2013903304

Any people depicted in stock imagery provided by Thinkstock are models,
and such images are being used for illustrative purposes only.
Certain stock imagery © Thinkstock.

This book is printed on acid-free paper.

Because of the dynamic nature of the Internet, any web
addresses or links contained in this book may have changed
since publication and may no longer be valid.

CHAPTER 1 – TODAY, SEPTEMBER 12 [2011]

///

THE TIME IS SUCH that the United States of America is in a state of uncertainty.

The upper echelon of government cannot collectively decide what the best method is toward a progressive way of living for the people they were put in office to represent. We (the USA) are under the leadership of this country's first formally inaugurated African-American (Black) President, Mr. "Floyd Boston" and it seems as though his constituents (both parties, Democrats and Republicans) don't want to see him succeed at guiding this country back to its number one world renowned status. The old days and ways of some of the people of this country still stand in the way of progress (Some things in this country will never change completely). Although, Mr. Boston inherited the discombobulated mess of the Toney Harris administration; he still stands defiant and most confident that he can turn this country around and I truly believe he can. The way he walks and talks gives me the confidence that one day I will live in a better America. I am not saying this because I am black; his bold approach and charismatic appearance tells me that he stands for everything I believe in about America. My belief is that it was not a mystery or coincidence how Mr. Boston came to power. This is my belief and I will always stand behind it. He (President Floyd Boston) was put into power intentionally by both political parties (Democrats and Republicans) because the reputation of the United States throughout the world was severely damaged by the Harris Administration and the only way to regain the world renowned political status the United States once secured was to put a Black man into power. Both parties knew that Austin Gray would be no match for Floyd Boston. Both parties knew that Austin Gray had about a snowballs chance in the Sahara Desert of defeating Floyd Boston. Mr. Boston played the game very well too. He (Mr. Boston) set back in Congress and watched nearly everything that was going on (the money corruption and mistress scandals prevalent in both parties) then Mr. Boston conversed with Mr. Alex Newton and the race to the presidential seat was on. When he (Mr. Boston) won the Iowa electoral votes I knew that he would become the next president of the United States. I have six brothers and we talk about this stuff all the time and I told them, man, when the state of Iowa say that a black man needs to be president then you can best believe that will be your next president. Sure enough that is what happened. At that time the state of Iowa was less than one percent black by population (and it could have been less than that). Yea, I said, when that many white people decide that a black man should be president, therefore you can best believe that is what is getting ready to happen. That is how I knew who would be the next president after Toney Harris. Both parties also thought Mr. Boston was going to be just another "Cotton Picking Yas'su Joe", but he turned the tables. He and Vise President (Mr. Alex Newton) now stand most defiant as to what America truly stands for (One Nation under God). I believe that Mr. Alex Newton truly believes in the fact that as Blacks and Whites together we built this country to the status of number one in the world as we held for many decades and that we will hold that status again, very soon. Yet, there be a few that think that this country was built alone by themselves (God bless them, I am always praying for them too). The president visited the Freightliner truck manufacturing plant in Mount Holly NC in March of 2012. I was employed for a cleaning contractor (CIS of NC) that cleans for Freightliner. Although, I was not allowed to attend the event at the plant, I had a chance to see his motorcade ride by within a few feet of where I was standing along the highway. I held my two year old nephew Anthony Jr. on the back of my neck. The scene was truly awesome; it was the most exciting event I ever witnessed, except for the birth of my son. I was interviewed by a local newspaper (The Charlotte Observer) and I told the reporter that one legacy of the president would be that he took the time to come to a small town like Mount Holly to check on the common working man. The entire event was just amazing!

Today, is the day after the 10th anniversary of the 9/11,2001 terrorist attacks of the World Trade Center towers in New York City ,USA (and, I think it's ironic that ten years afterwards the day itself would fall on a Sunday, the Christian Sabbath day) and that is pleasing to me. I feel there will never be anything to celebrate on that day (I feel the day should be called The Day of Mourning 9/11) and that is just my thoughts and understanding of it. I attended a church service that Sunday and the service was dedicated to the remembering of the lives taken on that horrible morning. I stood and spoke to the congregation as to my feelings about the attacks. I told them that I served in the United States military in order to stamp out the types of evil inflicted on our country that day. I served in order that my son, grand-daughter, nephews, friends, loved ones, and other American citizens could live without the fear of bombs exploding in their back yards or while shopping at a mall. I also told them that if they always acknowledged God through Jesus Christ that they would never have to walk around in life in fear. I also told them that they should be thankful (to God, through Jesus Christ) to men such as myself and all the other men and women that serve or have served in our military that they and their family members can lie down at night and get a peaceful night sleep. After the attacks I vowed not to live out the remainder of my life in fear of anything, except God, through Jesus Christ. I would not hesitate to serve in the military again, because I believe in the cause and I will die for any cause that I feel is great enough to believe in and I believe in freedom.

Today has been a quiet and subtle day. There is almost no breeze to rustle the trees lining the road in front of the house I presently dwell in. The air is still, the sun is shining bright, and the temperature is at a comfortable level. There are no breaking news reports of tragedy as relating to 9/11 and that is very soothing to me. I have not really watched the news broadcasts in the past few days because the news these days can be very heartbreaking. Killings happen like it is rabbit, quall, or deer hunting season, especially in Charlotte, North Carolina. It is truly surreal. Charlotte is surely not the only area of the country seething with criminal activity though. At this day and time there is a slew of horrific crimes carried out seemingly by every continuous movement of moments. It all seems chaotic. Everybody seems to want their particular agenda up front and foremost. The mode of this country today is that anything goes and if I or my group is not being heard then I/we need to cause trouble to be heard. More and more people are coming forth to promote their (strange agendas). The people of this country are beginning to believe that whatever they promote is right. No one is considering the children that are growing up and watching keenly most of the nonsense that is going on in America today.

I am writing this book with no direct disrespect to any particular group or individual. I am just calling the shots as I witness them develop before my very eyes. I will only speak my voice as to the reality of what I see, hear, read, and understand.

The newest trend of group promotion is the notion by gay men and women that is alright to openly and publicly display their sexual preference. Again, I mean no direct disrespect toward anyone. Nevertheless, what kind of example is that setting to the children of our future generations? I say this because I saw and read the article where in Washington DC (Our Capital) two women ministers (head church representatives) were standing close together beside two gay men elated about the possible right to get married. "Come on"! Where are we going America? The most troubling of bizarre occurrences is when I was watching the news broadcast a couple of months ago and some toy maker has made a baby doll that will allow two, three, and four year old little girls to breast feed. That is completely unacceptable from my view point. A two or three year old child should have absolutely no understanding of how to breast feed. Point blank. Also, the Casey Anthony case in Florida, I thought it to be one of the most ridiculous decisions the judicious system ever concluded. I pray always that the true killer/ killers of that defenseless two year old child will truly receive their reward (in this life and the one to follow). The Casey Anthony case was no different than the O.J. Simpson trial (I truly believe them both to be guilty) even so, I am not the judge. The true judge will have his say one day. There are certainly many more bizarre events occurring across our nation such that I would not have enough time left in my own life to speak of it all. Finally, there is one more case I would like to mention. The case was in Gastonia, North Carolina. Two young (black men) age twenty three were on trial together for supposedly killing a young pregnant black girl that was pulled into the line of gun fire by her boyfriend. The two men were found guilty and both were sentenced to *LIFE* in prison without the possibility of parole. This case happened about three or four months ago. The incident was supposedly gang related. The young girl and the baby died. I was truly devastated, mostly for the ignorance involved and the loss of four more young black people. The thought of two young men going to prison for the rest of their lives (at age twenty three), was just overwhelming to me. I saw some of the news coverage of the case after the guilty verdicts was handed down and both sides of the families were crying out in grief.

I went back in my memory of the drive-by shootings that plagued California in the 1990's and to a poem I wrote in 1994 surrounding those horrific events. My focus of the poem, as you will see is an exact reflection of what is continuing to happen within the black race and in neighborhoods around the country. The poem is called Drive By.

"Drive By"

1. Man fights woman, Boy fights girl – I wonder what's happening in our ongoing World.
2. A woman travails in pain with fear; her baby's birth is very near- A doctor spanks the ass, a baby's birth comes to pass, but why? Will he only grow up to be part of another Drive By?
3. Kids skip school trying to be cool- Do you not know my child that without learning you'll only become a fool.
4. Parents let their kids grow up wild- Then they cry when murder charges are filed.
5. For money, Jeeps, precious gold, and sale'in dope; men take from one another and destroy their own brother's soul.
6. There are colors of orange, yellow, pink, and blue- Why let the white get next to you.
7. With Love, hope, and peace we can stop these

troubles if Today we try- and maybe tomorrow we can stop the next Drive By.

Written and arranged: Wed. 7/6/1994
By: Terry Lee McClain

My question is, parents when are you going to take back your household and the parents run the kids, not the kids run the parents?

My focus and purpose of writing this book is to perhaps guide the upcoming children in a different direction through life. Different than the awkward path I have taken thus far in my own life. The internet has become a tool of evil that is allowing children and adults to engage in activities far beyond what it was intended for. The internet has become the gateway to all manner of evil. The mind set of society today is that it's alright to do any and everything and it is suppose to be acceptable-NO, most of what is going on at this day and time is NOT acceptable. And my voice is to the parents. Control what goes on in your household and maybe the next news report will not headline your child. Take back what is rightfully yours (your household).

Today, I am encased in my own set of troubles; I am unemployed and broke, yet I will not give in to pity or despair. Even in the midst of my numerous troubles I will trust in the Lord always and continue with this book, I cannot look back now. Therefore, today has been a good one and I know the next will bring the same but in a different form; because yesterday is gone and tomorrow will never come, because we are always in today.

CHAPTER 2 – THE PATH

I HAVE COME TO the understanding that life is carried out on a path. The path I am speaking of is the path that each and every individual that has ever lived must take. The path through life; my path is not like your path and your path is not like mine. I cannot tell you how to walk your path and you cannot tell me how to walk my path. Each and every person living has a different path. You cannot tell me how to clear the brush out of my path when you have brush lying in your path. My path has taken many twist and turns. There has been trash of my own that has littered my path, trees have fallen, and people have stood in my way; yet, every breath I take I continue to clear my path. All paths (yours and mine) will always end with death. Death awaits the travelers of every path. It has been this way from the beginning and it will be that way at the end. Therefore, destiny lies within the power of self and how self is determined to clear its path. The moral here is that success is achieved only by how well one keeps his or her path cleared.

To the young of society today I say; I see a lot of

danger in your paths. It seems to me that the parents of today have strayed away from clearing their paths from the times of old and have allowed the way of their children's paths to become difficult to clear. I tell you, you cannot look at how your parents have walked their path; you must find a way to clear your own path. Your path is cluttered with peer pressure, influence from bad friends to try drugs and alcohol, temptation of sex, bulling, and influence from violent video games. I tell you; you do not have to walk your path with anyone! Always know that God has your back and He will *NEVER* leave you. I stand in the middle of my own path now and I look around and I really don't know what to do next. Yet, I do know what to do. I know I can't do anything until I start. I must clear the debris before me. You will always have some debris to clear as you continue to live. Think about what I have spoken of. Also, You have no friends in the streets. The streets are undefeated and will always stay undefeated. Trust me or try it for yourself and I guarantee you will have a zero in the win column at the end of your street career.

Walk your path with pride and sureness; always keeping the faith (find something to believe in besides yourself), really look around yourself right now and see if there is anything you see that you actually created. And Never let anyone tell you that you're less than "Great", for you are just that; Great. Always remember that nothing outside of you can affect or determine what you really are within. Also, let no one judge you because of your skin color. You can become anything you want to be in this life, because God said, He would have not one of them to fail; therefore, that includes you. Thus, if your path is cluttered with the debris of life; stand and look around you for a minute, grab a rack, borrow a chainsaw from a neighbor or any other tools you can use and get to work. Your path will never get cleared until you start.

I continue to work on clearing my own path and will never give up or stop believing that one day I will have my path cleared just like I want it. I will always believe in one of many quotes of my own (" No circumstance nor quagmire can define who you truly are. Only you can ultimately define who you become.")Therefore, the above is the primary reason for writing this book. My path began June 18, 1963.

CHAPTER 3 – HOW WE GOT HERE

///

I DON'T KNOW HOW earth and everything existing around me got here. All I do know is that I am here and through reading, experience, and knowledge of existence around me; I have come to an understanding of how we got here- in the United States of America as a black people and psychologically perplexed race. My understanding of it all can be challenged, redefined, and reputed by whoever observes the forthcoming; it is of no matter to me. This is the way I have understood it and this is the way I will bring it to you.

Slavery took place around the world long before slavery came to America. The wars between the African people produced prisoners of those wars; and slaves. Therefore, my descendants were involved in those wars as well as yours (as a person claiming African descent). As time progressed the different tribes accumulated more and more prisoners. Eventually, the prisoners were traded to the white man for better weapons(guns) to fight other tribes; prisoners were also traded for food, cloth, and wine/rum (as described from the World Book Encyclopedia) the year published and volume I know not at this time. I do know I recorded a large section of the volume by hand and still have the word for word recordings in my possession. All I know is that I began recording under ("Black Americans"). Therefore, through trading and by capture our ancestors were hauled onto large ships and transported across the ocean like animals to the United States of America. To my knowledge and understanding that is how we got here. I look today at how the famines and wars have affected the living conditions in Africa and I am glad that I live in America. I love my ancestors with a passion and yet I feel like I would not want to be a part of what is going on there at this day and time. I love the American life style; although, I do not like the structure of law in the area of North Carolina where I now reside. Thus, today no one (black people) can use the excuse of the slavery days to justify their position in life. The opportunity for success and a better way of life is at its greatest height for black people at this day and time. Black people just need to eradicate the jealousy that has been embedded in their hearts toward one another during slavery and develop a mental understanding of (love thy neighbor as thy self) then as individuals we can achieve almost anything the heart desires.

To the young black people between 12 and 29 I say, stop taking the life of your brother. Don't let the past life of your parents or any other negative people surrounding you dictate how you live out your life. Check this, 300 years have passed as of 2012 when a British man(white man) from the West Indies came over to America with a letter (*The Willie Lynch Letter : The Making of a Slave*) he had written for the slave owners; telling them how to control their slaves. Even though, he brought a way for the slave owners to control their slaves; the man never knew that in the letter he was delivering, he was giving away the solution to the speech. I read the speech and I found the solution. He said; if a phenomenon does not happen and they see the light (Black PEOPLE) Then the cycle of his idea for controlling slaves would continue for 300 years and he even said, forever. The light he is speaking about (black men) is the reversal of the black male role in society. Today, the letter Willie Lynch wrote and spoke to the slave owners about is an undeniable reality. As I speak. *Look at the role of the black man today and reality should slam you on your back. It is Sad.* The black man has taken on the role of the woman; washing clothes, cooking, and waiting hand and foot on their women (some black men are just not standing up as real men). The black man is becoming extinct; not standing up in the church and not keeping family unity. The attitude of the black woman's quest to be independent makes me sick to the very core of my soul. Some black women act as though they don't need a descent black man and as though there's no descent black men left in this country. Truly, I mean no disrespect to black women; I love black women and believe that you're one of God's greater creations. I am merely saying that black women should also read the Willie Lynch Letter to absorb a better understanding of their true role for the black man and discontinue the role intended as described in the Willie Lynch Letter. Therefore, I say, and wish to incorporate the phrase and perhaps one day be the founder of the organization (Men Becoming Men Again).

I will not tell you the personal impact that the Willie Lynch letter had on me, I am going to give *You* the chance and opportunity to Study it for yourself. Look up the letter and view it for yourself. I cannot tell you everything and I am not going to. It is like the Bible, you have to read it for yourself and take it from there. Look at the Willie Lynch letter and then decide where you need to go from there. Go ahead, and look it up on the internet, read it and see if I am joking. Again, look it up; I already know that most of you are familiar with the internet. I am only saying, look at the light; it is trying to shine for you to see. The very light Willie Lynch didn't *Ever* intend for you to see. Guess what? I am one of the phenomenon's he spoke of; if you would only hear my voice. Find something that will give you a good reason to build and carry out a respectable life. You will never find a good life running the streets; because, again, the streets are undefeated and for the remainder of existence they will remain undefeated. You do not have any friends in the streets. The (so called friends) only want you to stay a part of the misery they are living in. I tell you these things from experience and not from what I have heard. See, you are already behind educationally and my theory for it is that when your ancestors (Black people) were held back from attending school in order to help in the fields; the white man was sending his children off to school. Therefore, obtain your education and find a way to understand a newer meaning as to why you are here on earth and the purpose behind the next breath you take. Always know that I believe that you are the next great person and never let anyone tell you that you cannot succeed and never let your skin color make you feel as though you are any less worth than the next person you see (black, white, blue, or green).Period.

I am in no way, form, or fashion prejudice and I have no ill feelings toward white people or any other race for that matter. My daddy (God rest his soul) was as black as any of the Africans you see on the "National Geographic's" channel and to me it seemed as though he had more white friends than black friends. I learned an invaluable lessen from his dealings with white people. I came to understand that the color of a person means absolutely nothing if that person has a good heart, a good spirit, and respect for his fellow man. So, I am not just talking black talk in this book. I speak to all. For, I would love to see all men get along. Therefore, I have spoken the above for the forthcoming reason. Hey! Young black people; In case you didn't know; school was not assembled for you to like or dislike, it was assembled to elevate your ability to think on a higher level and to give you a chance to develop skills in order to produce resources for your existence and survival here on earth. Wow! Yea, we got here on the bottom of ships, but from what I see of the mental condition of some of the young black males at this day and time; I don't know where we (black people) are going. Hey! They build yachts now and you can ride on top of the ship. The ultimate focus here is now that you know how you got here, where are you going? I am only hoping that the white people don't put us all on one of those Japanese trains that travel at 300 miles per hour and tell the engineer to set the controls to "Do Not Stop".

You will perhaps understand the meaning of what I have spoken above as the rest of this story unfolds. If you do not get it from here or by the end of this book, then I can only place your present care and the remainder of your existence here on earth in the care of the creator of time.

CHAPTER 4 – THE ILLUSION

I HAVE COME TO understand clearly the life in which I live and the existence of life around me. My mission for this story is that I save at least "One"; one black child from the hurt, pain, and misery of making multiple bad decisions up to and after becoming an adult (after age 21) for men and (after age 18) for women. My writings here are to perhaps get you to the age of 21 and beyond. Again, I write in hopes of inspiring children of all races. Although, At this point in my life I am more compelled to focus on young black people, because I feel that it is this particular group of people that are in the most critical mental situation and may only need positive guidance.

The illusion that I am speaking of is the illusion that there is no reality to life. That you already have all the right answers to everything. To the young black guys I say, life is like the performance of a magician; he is trying to make you believe that what he is performing is real, when in truth what he is performing is not real; (an illusion). There are many types of illusions that the world will show you. For one, that you can deal drugs and gain most of the material things you desire. Trust what I am telling you; it is not going to happen. The law is real and they are never going to allow you to deal drugs and live like a king (not in America) and especially a black man; you are living an illusion. Also, that it is alright to stop going to school in order to run the streets; let me tell you again that the streets are undefeated and will always remain undefeated. Also, you do not have any (true) friends in the streets. Your friends in the streets are only your friends because they want you to remain in the misery that they are wrapped in; again, (an illusion). Hey guys! Like I said in this story earlier, you do not have to carry out your life like your parents or other close members of your family. Alcohol (used in excess) and drugs will destroy your attempt to survive this life. Point blank. I have been there and done that. Finally, it is all an illusion. See, if you notice, I have said the same things more than once; it is because most everything about learning how to live and survive this life is about repeating the same things over and over.

To the young black females I say, you also live in the illusion that the young guys that you are getting involved with are the guys of your dreams and having kids by them. Let me tell you that most of the time these guys do not want you; all they want is what is below your belly button. After you have their baby they find a way to leave you and you become the next conversation when they get with the "boys" or talk over the phone to their friends; an illusion. Do you not feel like your life is worth more than being left with children without a daddy and becoming the next conversation of a group of guys. I am just saying; Think about what you are doing ladies. Use protection until you have a stable financial status (have a solid foundation in life) and then you can have as many babies as you want.

I do not have all the answers for everything, but I do see things among the young black people that if continued will not make them a better people in the future. And for the love of God! Stop believing that you can actually live like the rappers, the people in their videos, and the music they create. Some of these people have real families and real college degrees. Think about it, do you really think that the real law is going to allow you to ride around in1964 impalas and shoot at innocent people? Do you see the illusion in all of this? Finally, my brothers, search or find out the meaning of " love thy neighbor as thyself" and just in case you do not know who your neighbor is(in the previous phrase); Well,(I am sighing), I am going to tell you; your neighbor is every human being you will come in contact with the remainder of your life. See, I believe that as humans we represent the creator of existence through the many forms of our appearance. Thus, young black brothers, stop killing your neighbor (you do not have to prove anything to anybody) 25 to 30 years or life in prison is never going to be worth the 2 or 3 seconds of excitement just to see the power of a gun to impress your friends or to have a name in the streets. Add it up or compare the numbers and see for yourself if they will match. Again, it is never going to be worth it. I have my own faults and truly I have made mistakes along the way in my own life, but I do know today the difference between what is real and what is an illusion. Look at the change of seasons. When the leaves fall from the trees in the fall the trees appear to be dead and Spring brings the leaves and green grass right back to life (An illusion by the forces that control all things living and dead). Do you really think the trees and grass go through their changes by accident? No, it happens because there is a reality to existence; a reality that there are real forces in place controlling the things that cannot be seen by the naked eye. So, I say to you, take another look from here as to what you are really dealing with. Therefore, search out your own reality as to why you may exist and dig deep within to find a better meaning as to why you live and what is it that you are here on earth to represent. I believe in you and I hope you find a better meaning for living than the radical groups like the Taliban that train to take on suicide missions. I do not understand these types of groups, because there is no way I would let someone talk me into strapping a bomb to my chest and actually exploding it. I don't believe a man can create enough spit in his mouth to talk me into exploding a bomb strapped to my chest; even if he had a faucet screwed into his back and a hose pipe running up into his neck and the water supply was coming from the bottom of the Pacific Ocean. Unt'unn, No way you could talk me into that! A man just couldn't get his tongue wet enough. Excuse me for that last comment; I have always believed that a little laugh will never harm you. Finally, my young people; it is my hopes and prayers that by the end of this story you will have a clear or better understanding of my writings and truly know the meaning of the illusion I speak of.

CHAPTER 5 – MY BEGINNING

MY LIFE ON EARTH began on June 18, 1963. I was born in Shelby NC and grew up in Kings Mountain NC. My mother (I will always prefer to call her Moma) has often told me about my earlier childhood. Of many stories she keeps one in mind seemingly the most. She told about an incident that happened when I was an infant. I apparently had asthma at the time, had an attack one day, and could not breathe. She rushed me to the hospital in my daddy's 1967 Ford that had worn out brakes that had not been changed. She said, on the way to the hospital the only thing she could say was "Lord" don't let these brakes fail me. She said that all the way to the hospital the brakes worked fine and nearly all the way back until she turned into the drive way and that is when the brakes gave out. The only way she could stop the car was to run into a tree in our yard. She said it scared her nearly to death. The car stopped without causing too much damage to the front end and we were alright and for her that was all that mattered. She said that I was never bothered with asthma again since that day. My mother believed at that time and still believes to this day that it was no one but the "Lord" (Jesus) that was with us that day. She and I laugh about it every now and then to this day and each time she tells me the story it gets funnier and funnier. She is always fully convinced that the "Lord" applied the brakes when she needed them and protected us from any harm all the way to and from the hospital. I know now as a man that there is something out there (some force or forces) far beyond earth and far beyond what our minds can ever understand as human beings.

As I was growing up along with my brothers; Charles, Rogers, Timmy, Roydell, and eventually Anthony there was many other childhood experiences that are very laughable about today. I will always remember the "Tahzan Vine", it was a small (widened out in a circular fashion) body of water attached to a creek that ran through some woods not far from where we lived. I, my brothers, and kids from the surrounding neighborhood (from families like Hager, Oates, Womic, Walls, Herndon, and others that my mind cannot bring forth as of now) went to this creek often to swim (often without our parent's permission). It was our swimming pool. Somebody tied a large rope to a tree limb that hung out perfectly over the area of water we all splashed and swam in. We would swing out over the water from the rope and drop into the water. We could also dive in from the slippery rocks that the water ran over into the pool like a waterfall with a two to three foot drop off. That is why we all called this place (this Special Place) the "Tahzan Vine". The place actually looked and had the feel of the jungle scenes from the television show called "Tarzan". We all had a lot of fun there and it is one place I will never forget about as long as I live. I want you to know at this point that I am writing in the dialogue of the basic way of talking in the area I grew up in and that is why Tahzan is spelled the way it is and not like the actual spelling of the show called Tarzan. Some words spoken by some black people (absolutely no disrespect toward black people, it is just the way we are, we sometimes use the least amount of words to get something said) may not even be close to being spelled like the actual word and may have a total different meaning than the meaning of the actual word. I have also choose to write this story in a simple manner and form that the true understanding will not be lost to complex words; so that the most basic or complex mind will be able to understand. Believe me, I can go complex with words. And there is another dialogue of that time (during the time I was growing up and earlier) that is unknown to most of the world.

I also must not fail to mention the days of "West Shelby". Ahhh, those were the days! They were good and bad. I remember going to my grand-mothers house (The late, Moma;Dorenda) nearly every weekend and playing in and around the streets. I and a lot of the neighborhood kids would play all kinds of games from basketball to football (real tackle with no pads) to a game we use to call "Sneeky Fleeky". Sneeky Fleeky was a game that we played on the town drunks. We would wait until night fall and go to a house where we knew where men lived that had been drinking alcohol all day and we would knock on the door of the house and then run around the side of the house or behind a bush. The drunken men would answer the door to find no one there and after we would knock again and again the drunken men would come to the door and start cursing something terrible, I mean something awful. We would start laughing like crazy and run off to the next house. We played this game often to the point that the drunken men caught on to what we were doing and would not come to the door. The memories will always be with me. While we played the grown-ups were gambling (playing cards or pulling tip boards), drinking (alcohol) and fighting. It was an every weekend gathering at different houses and the results were always the same (family members fighting) then making up and drink together again. Man, those were the good ole days for real!

I also must mention a teenage girl friend (Ann) that I will never forget. I was twelve or thirteen when we met. She lived in "West Shelby" and we loved each other. I foolishly gave her away by introducing her to my best friend and later they became boyfriend and girlfriend. Their relationship bothered me for years and I have never gotten over it. To this day I will always regret that the forces whom control the elements of this world did not allow us to be together. We were just too young to know what we really had at that time (young love, compassion for each other, and the utmost respect for each other).

CHAPTER 6 – HIGH SCHOOL DAYS

██

THE GOOD OLE DAYS continue. The days of High School were some of the most exciting days of my life thus far. I went to Kings Mountain High School; graduated in 1981. I was a quiet low key kind of guy. I didn't have many friends and the ones I had I can call friends to this day. The late Calvin was the best of all my friends. He was a funny black guy that didn't take anything off anyone and would not let anybody mess with me. Thus, I had all the protection in the world from anyone that even thought about bullying me. I had other friends as well (Bernard, Kenny, Robert, Donald, Connie, Douglas, Billy, Dianna, Markus, David, Henry, Daron, Micheal, Tina, Frankie) and a few others I have not mentioned, but I mean no disrespect to anyone that I didn't mention above. The memories of those days in the late 1970's will always hold a memory of a high school sweetheart (Deborah). I had to fight with other guys (mentally) to convince them and her too that I was the guy for her. And finally I convinced her. We were boyfriend and girlfriend for five years; then something changed. Before I proceed forward I must go back and tell of my wrestling days and moments.

I was a superb wrestler under coach Moffit. To my recollection I was 56 and 5 as for wins and losses. I went to the NC State Regionals and lost in the first round due to a difficult call by the referee at the end of the match. Mr. Moffit was furious and yet the referee would not overturn his call. I lost and Mr. Moffit comforted me and told me not to worry about it, that I would surely be back next year and I truly believe he was sincere and really believed in me enough for me to believe that I could come back next year and even win the State Title. My chance never came. Although, I did defeat the eventual State Champion that year (1980) 3 to 2 in a home match against Ashebrook High School of Gastonia NC- which was my best match ever. I did not wrestle my senior year of high school. There were other problems going on in my life at home that I felt that was more important than my wrestling career. Mr.Moffit nearly begged me to wrestle my senior year; he even told me that he could possibly get me into Clemson University of South Carolina. I really believed I was good enough to get in at Clemson; even to this day I believe Mr. Moffit was truthful and was truly interested in my well being. Mr. Moffit was a super man (white man) and he being white did not once deter him from coaching a majority black wrestling team. Nor was he ever biased toward his wrestlers. I enjoyed wrestling because it took my mind away from being at home with alcoholic parents. I and 5 brothers lived in run down houses(usually two bedrooms along with no indoor toilet, no running water, rats, and roaches) we had to draw up water from a well. I and my brothers also had to draw the water to sloop hogs. Wrestling took me away from all the concerns of living at home. Therefore, I became very good at wrestling.

I only played one year of football. After I figured out that I did not want to try stopping a tailback named Kevin (whom went on to the NFL to play for the Cleveland Browns) and that I did not like the noise in my helmet when you collide with another player; that was enough football for me. I could not wait until the season ended so I could tunnel a path under the field house so I could leave my entire uniform under it. Although, I did inherit a nickname from my best friend (the late Calvin), he called me "Dirt" after the linebacker from the Pittsburg Steelers named "Dirt Winston", The nickname is still with me to this day (known only by a few old friends). I got the name by getting down and in the dirt to tackle somebody when I did get the opportunity to play (mostly in practice). The late Calvin named me "Dirt" and he called me by that name up until he died (GRHS). I realized football just wasn't for me, End of story and the end of my high school days.

CHAPTER 7 – THE TURNING POINT

I WAS SIXTEEN YEARS old when I went to work on my first full-time job in a cotton mill (McBess Industries) of Bessemer City NC. My uncle (the late Rudolph) got me the job and I was very happy to be working. After high school I continued to work. The job offered the opportunity for a lot of over-time hours and my life took off like a jet launched from an aircraft carrier. My first car (a black 1972 Chevy Malibu) and eventually my most prized of all the cars I've had (a White 1976 Monte Carlo). After I got the Monte Carlo I moved out from my parents. I just wanted a better way of living. I was steering toward wealth and success at supersonic speed. Everything was going my way; my credit was excellent, had my own apartment with new furniture throughout and new clothes in my closet with the purchase tags still on them. There was nothing seemingly I wanted for nor was there anything I couldn't get (materialistically). I believe today that at that time I had the world in the palm of my hand and just didn't know it. Also, the fall after high school I enrolled at Gaston College of Dallas NC as a full-time student in the field of Mechanical Engineering Production, at that time the field of study was named as such; today it is named Mechanical Engineering Technology. I had a girlfriend (Deborah) that I was in love with. We had a beautiful relationship and her family members were very fond of me as well. We went to church together; we were together constantly. As I said, life could not have granted me a better outcome, I had the world in the palm of my hands. I also said earlier that something changed. I know what happened today, I just didn't understand my actions at that time. Today I understand that life was going so well that I became complacent as to be grateful for the things I already had and I wanted to change women to demonstrate that I was moving up in life. That is what happened to separate me and Deborah. And if she ever reads this story I will always want her to know that I am sorry for what happened between us and that I love her (through Jesus Christ). I also, ask for her forgiveness. What happened between me and Deborah was a turning point that changed the course of my life; perhaps till the day I die.

As I said, we were in love and happy together until I met another girl while at Gaston College (Tina). The very first day I saw her I knew that I wanted her (I had to have her at any cost). Me and a friend at that time (Ken) was hanging out, shooting a game of pool in the College game room that was on an upper level floor. I looked out the giant window and down below I saw her (Tina) walking by with one of her friend girls. Somewhere inside me I knew she was the girl for me. I got lucky on

April 12th 1982 when I was walking through one of the school corridors and saw her (Tina) sitting on a couch. I realized it was the perfect time to talk to her, because I had always been a shy type of guy that did not like to talk to girls when other people were around. We talked and exchanged phone numbers, I also asked her out for a date and she accepted. We started dating on a regular basis and later became boyfriend and girlfriend (I was the most happy ever I lived). I didn't know then, but that day I formally met Tina was the turning point that changed the course of my life until the day I die. I broke up with Deborah almost immediately. I went to her one night and told her that I was in love with somebody else. It crushed her to the core of her soul. I knew then and now I surely know, because I feel the pain now that I inflicted upon her and I never intended to. We were so close (she was the first girl I had sex with) and I destroyed our relationship in one night. That is what happened between Deborah and me. I truly believe that to this day neither of us has healed. I from causing the pain and she from receiving the pain I delivered. Years later I received the same pain from my wife(Tina) which I will not elaborate on for the sake of the respect I hold for her today as the mother of my only son(for today is all we have, yesterday is gone and tomorrow will never come).

My life changed directions as we (me and Tina) continued dating. I was still employed at McBess Industries when after four consecutive years to the very date I was hired, I walked off of my job due to a dispute with the plant manager over some yarn that was messed up by first shift and he (the plant manager) tried to blame everything on me (and I was not going for that and by this time in my life I had had enough of textiles) thus, I decided to pursue the field and career I was going to college for (Mechanical Engineering Production). I was determined to never work in another cotton mill.

It was another turning point in my life. Later, I found that prejudice was still running rampant in this country (USA) and I couldn't land that dream job in engineering. Therefore, my bills were piling up and my grades were sliding due to the stress and I was deeply in love with Tina. My brother (Roger) was in the Navy and suggested I join and at the time I was running out of alternatives (I didn't want my credit and upstanding reputation ruined) thus, I joined the military on Sept 27th 1984. I left my girlfriend (Tina) and received my orders to San Diego, CA.

Boot camp introduced total chaos to my mental ability to think. During boot camp I received a letter from Tina begging me to come back for her (in NC) and the letter smashed my heart so bad that I felt that I just couldn't leave her behind. Therefore, I wrote back and asked her to marry me, and she gladly accepted. When boot camp ended I flew back to NC and on Dec.23rd 1984 I and Tina were married. We didn't have an elaborate wedding due to our financial situation; yet we had a beautiful reception. We were happy, in love, and together; and that was all that mattered to us. I truly believe that she was happy because I didn't leave her behind after going into the military. I flew back to California to complete my training as an electrician for the Navy Seabees and she stayed in NC. Several months later I had her flown to California to join me. We stayed off base and were a mile or so from the beach. We went to the beach often and had the best of times together. I truly loved her, but during this time my buddies at the base got between our happiness (all my fault). The nights out partying with the guys, alcohol, and marijuana was a strain on our marriage. We stayed together although our marriage was starting to slip into collapse. It started to plunge toward destruction when I committed adultery. Our relationship was just never quite the same. Even so, she stuck by me and at the time I was thankful for that. God and Jesus Christ in heaven knows I loved her, and yet alcoholism had slipped its way into my life; unawares. She stayed with me up until my first scheduled deployment to Japan. I flew her back to NC in January 1986 to live with her parents (Mr. Issac and Mrs. Wyonia) of Dallas NC until I could make arrangements to fly her to Japan. The deployment or intentions to fly my wife to Japan never happened.

CHAPTER 8 – COMPLETE
DEVASTATION

THE MORNING OF JANUARY 3, 1986 was a beautiful, sunny, California day. I was standing in morning ranks during muster (when all companies of our unit meet to be counted) when without notice I was suddenly called out of ranks (I was caught totally off guard and said, what has happened now?) because I was taken to the Chaplin (I knew right then that something was not right) various things ran through my mind and then I thought about my wife (Tina). When I got to the Chaplin's office he handed me the telephone. I was nervous from the very beginning as I reached for the phone. I put the receiver to my ear (I don't remember if I was shaking or not) the voice was my wife and I released an instant sigh of relief. Although, I was relieved that the person on the other end of the phone was my wife, I still could feel that something was wrong and it was. My wife began to tell me of the fatal car accident involving her sister (the late, Phillis)(GRHS) whom was with child. The car crash happened as my wife was landing at Charlotte Douglas Airport in Charlotte NC. My wife was just returning home from living with me in California. I immediately felt the complete devastation through my wife, because I and Phillis were very close also. I talked with the Chaplin a few more minutes and told him that I was fine- although I was not. The entire chain of events had my mind in a tail spin. I eventually went to my commanding officer and requested to go home to NC in order to make sure that my wife was alright before going to Japan. My request was denied because we were days away from deploying and the military didn't count a sister-n-law as immediate family. I was destroyed inside and did not know what to do or know where to turn. Therefore, I went to the base liquor store and purchased a half gallon of Jack Daniels and a half case of Bud Wiser beer. I returned to my room on base and commenced to drinking. I stayed drunk for seven or eight day's straight, not eating much, not sleeping much. Finally, I lost touch with reality. My friend (Donald) tried his best to help me keep myself together and despite all his tiresome effort; it was too late. My feelings had collapsed; mind, heart, body, and soul. Again, everything around me was in complete devastation.

I went to quarters one morning (out of uniform; I had on the hard hat that we were to use on our deployment and quarters that morning called for a soft cover hat. Again, I was completely out of uniform). My company commander walked up to me and asked if I was okay? I said no I am not okay, Sir. He instructed me to go to the base medical center immediately. I went to the base medical center as directed and there saw a doctor. The doctor asked me if I was hearing voices and I said, yes. He asked me to describe the voices and told him that it was like everyone around me was either talking to me or about me all at once. That is what it is like to lose touch with reality. From my base in Port Hueneme California I was transported (that day) to the main Navel Hospital in Long Beach California.

I was questioned by someone- whom by I know not now. I was asked the same type of questions, was I hearing voices? Was I seeing things that were not there? I did not see strange things, but I was hearing voices. After a long wait I was escorted to a ward- I had no idea in the world what a ward was; I will always know now. Yes, I was taken to an insane asylum ward. Once on the ward I became very unsure as to what was going on. I was seated in a room and after a while two E- 2's (low ranking enlisted men) came in and started asking me all kinds of questions- I cannot begin to recall all the questions, by this time my mind is turning flips like a carnival ride. Then the unthinkable happened, I was immediately taken to a padded room (padded on all walls) and while standing in the door way the two E-2's told me to take off all my clothes (I mean, they told me to strip naked) and after a very lengthy consideration and the situation was looking more and more like if I did not strip the two E-2's were going to strip me by force. I did not know what to do and had no one else to turn to; I was in a quandary. Therefore, I stripped and handed one of the two all my clothes; they even demanded that I give them my dog-tags (dog-tags are the way the military identifies a person if found dead or if captured by the enemy during war). After a long hesitation I slowly removed my dog-tags and handed them over (to this very day I never saw my dog-tags again) they backed slowly from the door way and shut the door and bolt locked it seemingly several times. I am now alone and was alone for many hours (it seemed like days). My mind was racing like NASCAR drivers at Talladega, I began to think that if they took my dog-tags they were going to kill me and cover up everything. The only person that I knew in California (family wise) at this point was my wife Tina and now she was three thousand miles away in Dallas NC. No other family members at this point knew anything about where I was. It was all horrifying. I really flipped out in that room, I started seeing little green men on the roof of the floor below, running into the walls with my head and pounding on the door, yelling, and screaming to get out of that room, and I was being feed through a trap door like an animal (I felt like an animal). The situation turned worse because after many days of isolation in that padded room they came in and began to give me shots by force. The medicine did not agree with my biological chemical makeup (DNA) and the medicine sent me in a tail spin. I went through days in that room trying to stop the pain from muscle spasms (I was crippled to the point that I could not stop my right arm from rising over my head, my neck would turn literally like the girl on the movie The Exorcist, I was drooling at the mouth like a new born infant) the pain was truly excruciating. The pain was so severe that I just wanted to die. I was eventually given an overdose and stayed sleep for three days as told to me when I woke up and people was standing all around me. I was strapped to a gurney that the staff had to bring into the padded room in order to get me to know that I was in a real hospital and that they were not trying to kill me. After a few hours I was then moved to a room with four concrete walls, the room is called The Blue Room. It was named as such because the entire room is colored light blue. I immediately lost my mind in that room, I was out of touch with reality so bad that I was running into the concrete walls with my head, my head had knots all over the size of a quarter or larger. I was having horrific dreams of driving a huge bus and huge black spiders crawling up and down the blue walls. I was in such bad shape in the blue room that the staff finally figured out that the medicine (haldol & cogentin) was making me hallucinate. They found out also that the dosage they had been giving me was too high. By now my coordination was off so bad that I could only walk at the pace of perhaps a deteriorating 98 or 99 year old man. They took me out of the blue room several days later and put me in a padded room again. They eventually lowered the dosage of medicines although I was no better. One day while a nurse (a petit white woman) opened the door to hand me a tray of food and suddenly I stormed by her forcefully and snatched a leather strap off another locked door (to this day I do not know where the power or force came from to allow me to pull off such a feat) and eventually escaped from the ward and the hospital grounds. I ran up the highway, I ran and ran and ran until I was exhausted. I was running up a major highway in the city of Long Beach California. I became so frightened that I climbed up onto a bridge and was getting ready to jump beneath into the oncoming traffic of another major highway. And just when I was going to jump, something touched me on my right shoulder and I stopped and stood there in a solid stand still (I know now what that something was that touched my right shoulder, It was the angel of Spare Life sent by Jesus Christ himself and that is what I will always believe) – I believe some words are angels. I climbed down from the bridge and continued to run. I ended in the uptown area asking people to help me. I was in hospital pajamas and bare footed. Finally, with nowhere to go I was surrounded by military police. They secured me and took me back to the hospital. They put me back in the padded room. Later, they got my medicines regulated well enough to let me out. Jan 28, 1986, the same morning the Space Shuttle Challenger exploded moments after takeoff. I was still a little out of touch with reality and did not believe that the Space Shuttle exploded like that. I had just spent 19 days isolated in a padded room and a blue room; and I just could not believe it (I have always been a Space Program fan), I just do not see why our government wants to spend hundreds of billions of our precious tax money just to see if a monkey can peel a banana in weightless space when there are so many problems here on earth, even as I speak. I saw the explosion on replay and I still did not believe it had happened. I was so in disbelief that I had to call my wife Tina three thousand miles away just to know if the explosion was real or not. I made the call from a phone booth on the ward floor. My wife did confirm for me that the explosion did happen and therefore, I had to believe it because I knew at that time that my wife was the only person living that would not lie to me because my wife knew how I loved the Space Program. While my wife and I continued to talk small talk the unthinkable started to happen. My neck started to turn and I couldn't stop it, my right arm began to rise over my head and my mouth began to lock itself to one side and spittle started to slowly slide out of the side of my mouth like a new born child. The pain was so excruciating that I told my wife I had to go and before we said I love you byes I dropped the phone and left it dangling by the cord. Another patient walked in the room and saw my condition and started yelling for help. The staff came and took me to my bed and immediately shot me in the hip with some medicine (cogentin), the pain from the muscle spasms was unbearable. I eventually absorbed the pain and went to sleep. The muscle spasms were due to the staff giving me more of one medicine than the other. The two medicines (haldol & cogentin) must be mixed properly in order to work sufficiently and they never could get the medicines mixed right for my nervous system. I believe to this day that the two medicines damaged a part of my brain that is irreversible. Since then I have not been able to put together a stable life (live as do normal people). I tend to go in and out of living a stable life, but I will never quit, I will never stop believing that my life one day will be normal like it was before I joined the military.

The hospital staff eventually told me that there was no more they could do for me and in my state of denial and confusion, they flew me by medivac to the Bill Heffner VA medical center in Salisbury NC. When I arrived I was examined by a doctor that told me that the hospital in California had been giving me the wrong medicines for the wrong problem; that I was suffering from severe depression. The doctor called out to the hospital in California and they told her that my records were burned in an accidental fire in the records room.

The doctor got off the phone and just laughed a little. She said to me, it's ironic that your records suddenly got burned up in a fire. The doctor put me on an anti-depressant and a month or so later I was ready to be discharged.

CHAPTER 9 – RECOUPING

THE DAY I LEFT the hospital I knew I had a long road ahead toward recouping and truly it was a long road. I moved in with my wife and her parents in Dallas NC. We all got along very well. I recouped well enough to eventually go to work as an electrician for a local company that made house trailers. The work was steady and I made descent money. I eventually made enough to allow for me and my wife to move out on our own. The first year went well and yet a problem existed. By now through my military experience I had become a steady alcohol drinker (beer mostly). I didn't know anything about alcoholism by this time (only from the experience of the drinking I witnessed of my parents and other family members) I never imagined that I was swiftly heading down the stream toward becoming an alcoholic. The drinking got worse and worse. My drinking got to the point of frequent separations with my wife. My wife was a good woman and I will never take those words back. The problem for us was me and within me. I got out of the hospital in June of 1986 and three years of so later in September of 1989 my wife left me and we were never again together in the same household as husband and wife. By now I had had a brush with the shoulders of the law (one DWI). I did not think much of the DWI when I got it because it was my first time ever being involved with the law and I pleaded guilty out right even though truthfully I was not driving the car. Nevertheless, I just blew it off as just a little mistake. That one mistake ignited the flame to an unintentional career of crime activity. When my wife left me in September of 1989 and took my only son Philip (one year old or so) it was the final thread that started the unraveling of my life (even today I have not fully eradicated the relentless pain of my wife leaving me at that time, and yet today it troubles me not at all, because time has changed along with the feelings of my heart). I did love her for every word of the meaning of love. My life plunged to a depth of darkness darker than the waters at the greatest depths of the sea. I became homeless, living on the streets of Gastonia NC and Shelby NC. I hung out with the drunks, wineo's, and crack users as though we were blood brothers (I did anything and everything they would do, except shoot up). I slept in abandoned buildings and ate the food brought back by the drunks and wineo's (never knowing or cared where the food came from). I was so far down in despair that it didn't matter if I lived or died. At this point I wanted to give up on life. I was hurt and unsatisfied that I could no longer be with the woman I truly loved (my wife Tina).

The morning I woke up in the abandoned trailer of an eighteen wheeler, I spoke to myself and said as though to my wife, if I did without you the last twenty-four hours then I can do without you the rest of my life (the light bulb had come on revealing to me that we would perhaps never live together as a family again). I got up and have not looked back on the marriage that we had. Today my ex- wife and I are divorced(since 1996) but have a good friendly relationship; along with my son Philip who is twenty-four(we have a great relationship) and a super aspiring rapper named META#4 and a very beautiful and unique three year old grand- daughter(Ariah) and her caring mother Sheree. Who can ask of greater blessings from God than I, life today is most grand for me.

I eventually moved my street experience to Shelby NC and by now (between 1989 and 1992 I had lost my driver license to three DWI's and my life truly had no meaning (I could not raise myself out of the valley of shame, self pity, and zero self esteem). I ran the streets with not one care if I woke up the next day or not; and, many nights I wished I would die during the night in order that I would not have to face another tomorrow (in my heart and soul I was destroyed; yet in my mind I could never completely give up hope that one day I could lead a better life). I am fully recouped to this day because I never gave up on my hope. I read a book many years ago called A Nickels Worth Of Hope (if you are still running the streets and want to live a better life one day, I strongly and Highly suggest that you find this book and read it in its entirety) it has preserved my life that I live to this day. I even keep a nickel in my wallet at all times to this moment. I will not tell you what the book is about, all I will tell you is if you choice to want to change your life for the better toward yourself and toward your fellow neighbor then find this book and read it for yourself.

Because, I tell you again (the young to the old) the streets are undefeated and they will never lose.

In 1993 while running the streets of Shelby NC I pulled three robberies of area convenience stores. I was with a street friend when I robbed the first store. I never had any intentions of harming anyone (because I have never really been the violent type) and yet I opened a very small pocket knife and pointed it toward the cashier (not knowing the law to the point that a pocket knife or a tooth pick was the same as having a double barrel shot gun when you attempt to rob somebody; a business or individual).When all the court proceedings were over I was sentenced to fourteen years in prison with ten years probation running after the fourteen years. I was truly blessed by Jesus Christ that at that time the law was fair to criminals; because, whatever time you were sentenced to and went to prison for, it was cut in half once you started your prison sentence and for good behavior you could even reduce the sentence more. I eventually did five and one half years from 1994 to April 1999. I was out of prison less than a month and did another robbery (with no weapons involved, I had learned that much at least from the previous prison sentence) and went to jail in Gastonia NC in May of 1999. I served eight more months in the county jail and was released in December of 1999. Three days before I got out of jail I had truly made a decision. I had talked with myself and said; the sinful person that was inside me had to leave, because the ways of the world was not going to change; I had to change. I left the jail and I did no alcohol or drugs for the next seven years (until 2006).

I relapsed in 2006 due to a heart attack and the

pressure of not being able to secure stable and descent paying work; due to my criminal background. Again, I went to prison for common law robbery and crack cocaine possession in 2009 and was released in July 2011. Today I am clean and sober once again and truly plan to stay that way until my days be ended on the earth. Young people, drugs and alcohol will destroy your chances to lead a better life; point blank.

I have been many places around the USA. I have been in mental institutions (throughout NC) more times than I can count (mostly in Veterans Administration hospitals). I have worked for Disney World of Orlando Flordia in 1990 as a train conductor in the Magic Kingdom, worked in sweet potatoes fields in Fuqua Varina near Raleigh NC in1990 (escaping in the middle of the night, alone, and with no money) I could not believe that black people were still in slavery (legally to themselves) in 1990. I just could not take beholding the humiliation of my people that I was witnessing. I have a dislike for sweet potatoes to this day. I have worked in all areas of industry from textiles to construction since age sixteen. I have run the streets in Winston Salem NC, Raleigh NC (leaving Raleigh due to being robbed and severely beaten one night while out drinking), Durham NC, Shelby NC, Kings Mountain NC, Charlotte NC and Gastonia NC. I have stayed at countless shelters. My path has been rough to travel and I suggest the street life to no one. Because, it is in your mind to be a better person; you just got to dig deep within yourself and believe that you are no different than any other human being.

Recouping from a broken life takes years to complete and yet it is never really completed, but it can happen.

You can recoup from almost any kind of trauma if you have the desire. Because, when you go through something rough, horrific or traumatizing you can look back one day and say; wow, that was not so bad. Today I have conquered the greatest obstacles that life can throw to a man and I am proud of myself. Today I am satisfied with my position in life and happy with basically all aspects of my life and it seems to be getting even better.

CHAPTR 10 – THE CHURCH

THE CHURCH IS IN trouble at this day in time. I believe in God the Father, Jesus Christ, and The Holy Ghost. My beliefs will never change. I believe that Jesus Christ has come to earth in the form of God and lived a sinless life and died on the Cross for the remission of all of mankind sins and rose on the third day and ascended to Heaven to reign on the right hand of God. That is my faith toward what I believe and I do not foresee that changing now or in the future. Not for you or any other human being. I am rooted and grounded in my faith toward Jesus Christ.

I am troubled with the church. I am taken aback that at this day in time people are using the church as a smoke screen to cover up their sinful ways and I know that God is not pleased with where His churches are. Jesus said in Matthew 7:15, Beware of false prophets, which come to you in sheep's clothing, but inwardly they are ravening wolves. People are promoting that literally any and everything goes in church (and it should not be such); people are proclaiming that they have the faith and are full of doubt (not truly believing that God exists). Talking about each other and stirring up slander at every turn. Jesus said; love thy neighbor as thyself. I am sorry; I just don't see a lot of the love toward one another as Jesus spoke of. Today, I just don't see it in the majority of people in the churches. Because, if you loved me you would not give up on me and talk about me; I am just trying to lead a better life just like the next person that is truly trying. But, one day God shall redeem His church; you can rest assured on that (true believers). I have read the Holy Bible completely through twice and read countless scripture passages (over and over) and I speak the truth; God shall come and redeem His church. The Holy Bible is the key to your every success; if you will only open your heart, repent, and never lay down your faith.

I wish to finish this chapter with my theory concerning God. The 3 in 1 Theory: Formula, $I = cMw$. For this theory, all letters have different meanings, but all represent the same numerical value of 1. Therefore, I = The physical and spiritual attributes of an individual along with his/her intellect.

c = The primary beginning of a human being or individual...Meaning a child or baby.

M = The latter dimension of a boy or child...Meaning a man.

w = The latter dimension of a girl or child...Meaning a woman.

Therefore, my theory is such: That there are only 3 personalities in 1 human being, and only 3. The child, the man, and the woman. I have seen the phenomenon over and over and over. I came to this profound theory after seemingly endless discussions with brothers of the Muslim religion (zero disrespect toward the Muslim religion here) and from mine own perception of existence around me. The brothers I have talked with do not believe in the possibility of 3 people existing in 1(God). Their concept of belief is that there is no way that the deity (God, Jesus Christ, and The Holy Ghost) can exist as 1 or was formed by 1 individual (God alone) and yet, have 2 other figures existing within Him (God), all at the same time or a 3 in 1 being. I am 49 years old, and as long as I have lived or came to understand life, I understand that a man and woman "must" have sexual intercourse to form a child; there must be a male and female mixture of reproduction fluids. And that is why I fully believe in the deity existing as 3 in 1. I truly believe that we are all individuals with 3 personalities in 1 being. We all possess the same basic characteristics; whether black, white, Mexican, or German. We all sleep, eat, and die. I fully believe too that we were all created by 1 being (GOD) or (I) in the formula for this theory. But, His reasons for creating people with minds like serial killers, violent rapists, child molesters, and mentally challenged people are truly beyond mine own comprehension. And ultimately, perhaps that is the way it was meant to be. We also act in basically the same manner. A child can act like an adult, a man can act like a woman or child, and a woman can act like a man or child. In all factual actuality we are all 3 in 1. The problem with people like serial killers, rapists, child molesters, and other violent dysfunctional members of our society is their inability to distinguish between which of the 3 personalities they really want controlling them. They allow 1 of the 3 personalities to fully dominate their mind so powerfully that they become deranged. Simply; the lack of mental balance. That balance of mind that makes normal people normal (if there is such a case as normal people). The ability to laugh and be silly like a child, keep priorities in order (work, husband duties, paying bills, etc...) like a man, and be able to cry, complain, yell, be cunning, and become broken hearted like a woman. I believe that doctors in psychiatry need to restudy the behavior of mankind on the basis presented here and proceed to help the aforementioned (true mental cases) by helping them equalize the mental unbalance of the 3 personalities. Help them to identify the 1 personality that affects them the most. Treat them by treating the 3 personalities, separately. Treat the child with child like subjects, the man with manly subjects, and the woman with womanly subjects. Thus, attempting to create an equal balance of the mind. This process could perhaps reduce multiple killings, domestic violence, and sexual violence in our society. Because, balance of mind is the essence, excitement, and honor of being human. Therefore, a future reduction in the above type of violent acts will eventually depend on developing this profound theory.

Derived by: Terry Lee McClain (2001)

Therefore, from ISAIAH 45:5-7, (5) I am the Lord, and there is none else, there is no God beside me: I girded thee, though thou hast not known me. (6) That they may know from the rising of the sun, and from the west, that there is none beside me. I am the Lord, and there is none else. (7) I form the light, and create darkness: I make peace, and create evil: I the Lord do all these things.

When you find the meaning of verse 7 you will find the key that opens the door to the treasures of heaven.

CHAPTER II – I HUNT

I HAVE LIKENED MY life to that of the Cheetah, or Hunting Leopard. I hunt. I hunt for a better way to live, I hunt the resources to survive, I hunt to get that money. I hunt opportunity, I hunt prosperity, I hunt for peace with all men, women, and children. I have hunted like a well hidden hunter. I have been hunting for many years. I have hunted for happiness all my days and captured it in Jesus Christ, I have hunted for a true soul mate, and I have hunted for my next day on earth to be a better one. I hunt every day of my life that I might capture joy and peace of mind, I hunt for respect from my fellow man as I also give, I hunt for that quality of life that makes life worth living, I hunt for my soul to be at peace with Jesus Christ. Yea, I have always hunted; even when it didn't appear so to others. I hunt that I may capture my next meal, I hunt to capture the beautiful pleasures that this life can give. I hunt that I may capture the excitement and pleasure of taking my next breath.

As of today Monday 1.14.2013, I reside in Mount Holly NC, I am retired from the military (USN Seabee's), happy within with joy and peace, and have a true soul mate. Today, I have a beautiful grand-daughter (Ariah) and Son (Philip), I am clean and sober, and have captured the resources to assure my future survival.

Unexpectedly and sadly, My daddy (Robbie) Whom I miss to this day died in October of 1999 of an apparent heart attack; may God rest his soul. He was a descent man, (for I call no man good or Father; for my Father is in heaven and Jesus said , there is none good but one, except my Father which is in heaven). My daddy was also a hunter.

My mother (Sally) still lives and stopped drinking (cold turkey) in 1984 and has not had a drink of anything since. Thus, I know it can be done from what I have seen from my mother. She never used A.A. or any other support group, but I will bet you she has a higher power; because I hear about Him all the time. As I said earlier, live out your own path through life, for it is the essence and beauty of living.

I have also had my driver license reinstated since 2004.They are in my wallet right now and don't expire until 2016 and that's where I intend for them to stay; in my wallet. I told my brothers that the next time they are taken I hope it is the coroner that takes them. I also told my brothers that if I was dropped in the middle of the Indian Ocean in only under wear, blue jeans, a ping pong ball, and a plastic fork I would return. They asked what the plastic fork and ping pong ball was for. I said, to fight off the sharks then eat them with the fork and to float with the ping pong ball till I get to shore. Me and my brothers joke around all the time.

I dropped out of Gaston College of Dallas NC in

1984 and returned in 2001, and graduated in 2003 in Mechanical Engineering Technology; then transferred my two year degree to UNC-Charlotte of Charlotte NC in 2004. I intend to return to UNC-Charlotte in August 2013 to continue my pursuit of a B.S. (Bachelor of Science) degree in Mechanical Engineering Technology. *You never ever give up on your dreams (or the prey you hunt).* Therefore, what more can a man bring home after many years of hunting, and all the days left of my life I will continue to hunt. Yea, I hunt.

What are you hunting for today? Come and hunt with me I might show you a skill or two. Peace, and continue to pray for me as I do for you and all others.

CHAPTER 12 – POEMS AND WORDS OF ENCOURAGEMENT

//

I WROTE THIS BOOK to inspire the young and aging and it is never too late for the old to learn. Now, I leave you with my poems and some words of encouragement: This first poem is dedicated to my mother (Sally).

"Mother"

Mother, I know the love you hold inside for the children you so painfully bared, but by growth, age, and unchangeable time they seemingly have greatly erred. The days of our lives are never the same and sometimes we wonder who is to blame; is it truly I who has wrought up all this dreadful shame or is it the one who created the being in my pain stricken frame? I have lived happy days and surely endured the bad and even now I am not so deeply sad. My love, feelings, emotions, and cares for you are deeply held within which no person, place, nor separation from sight can ever surpass... I only hope to embrace you again with a smile and say, Mother, this too shall pass. The man I am no one can understand, neither you, my brothers, nor the stranger at my left hand. The course of my life and the soft chambers of my heart have encountered great pain, which only words of sorrow could ever all explain. A now forgotten love that numbed my soul; leaving no feelings, care, nor concerns. My inward man even now lives beyond the creation of many needful tears. There is no way you could ever understand, that is why I have put all worries, cares, and concerns into Our Creators' hand. But my soul is at peace now; my happiness and joy comes from the one who started this unknown where to plan, because I know by faith He will never leave my right hand. Mother, I love you and there is no more I can explain, I only hope again to hold your loving hand... Mother, Mother, Mother; someday we will all understand.

Written and arranged by: Terry Lee McClain

"The Face of Joy"

Strong as a lion yet soft as the fur of a teddy bear. I see the inner strength as the body of a strong teenage boy. You know when to laugh, you know when to cry. Your loving heart repeats the same loving beats and you give from a well that is very deep within your soul. If I could dream the perfect dream and would see a beautiful human face, I would want to dream the face of you. And when I see your lovely face and remember all the great things you have taught me about life; that it is the little things therein that really matter and remember that you have labored so diligently to raise your young by faith in Christ alone and how you rush like the waves over the sea when a raging storm is roaring to help someone else in need, how you are happy with others during their triumphs and share your grief during their defeats. There is more good in you than the numerous small pieces of a large puzzle and my perfect dream of a woman would be complete. I would remember the dream always with a smile on my face like a boy receiving his first toy and I would be happy the rest of my life; because it was you I saw in that perfect dream and in seeing you, I saw the face of Joy.

Written and arranged by: Terry Lee McClain

"A Friend"

A friend to me is like a creature at the depths of the sea. When the world overshadows me with darkness, there with me you will be. When I am lonely and feel as though I cannot go on another mile, there you are with a happy and precious smile...A friend to me is like a rising sun, it shines in through a window to brighten up ones day. That is the feeling I get when I hear your voice and to me you just say, hey... A friend to me is like the beauty of a wedding that is done. The memory becomes embedded like the thrill and essence of watching children at play; they are filled with joy and seem to run, run, and run... A friend to me is like the light that ignites a flame; the precious glow begins, the warmth cuts through a cold winter night, and the song of creatures are always the same... But most of all, a friend will be there for you when the sun doesn't even shine, and today I hope you will be my friend and special Valentine!!!

Written and arranged by: Terry Lee McClain

"My Thoughts of You"

You remind me of the oceans color of blue, and sometimes there is no explaining My Thoughts of You. Diamonds and pearls are beautiful that is true, but nothing has a better shine than the smile on you. Out of all the things I have seen and of all the places I have gone, You are the only One I have seen that resemble the yellow rays of the sun. My Thoughts of You are like watching children play in the streets; they are laughing, they are happy to be free. And to me, watching you is better than watching a sunset by the sea.

Written and arranged by: Terry Lee McClain

"YOU"

I've been many places and saw many things, but nothing has ever caught my eye that looks quite like YOU. The way you walk and the way you smile as you talk, makes me think of a couple holding hands taking a late night walk. When I see your beautiful face, it makes me think of a quiet peaceful place. When I see you blush, it makes my heart speed into a steady rush. When I see a sunset by the sea and I stand to watch the awesome view, it only makes me think of seeing YOU. When I hear your voice, it makes me feel like I've bought something new, and I'm filled with happiness, because I know it can only be YOU.

Written and arranged by: Terry Lee McClain

"Just A Stare"

My memories of our past will forever last; now that you're gone my heart is so alone. Time can never pass away the love I have for you... I only need for you to love me too. My life is now spent in moments of despair which neither my heart nor soul are able to bear... That's why often I sit in Just a Stare. My days come and sadly go, with no comfort in my heart... I only wish the pain to stop and the love again to start. My mind often wanders here and there, saying there's no way this can be fair... That's why I often sit in Just a Stare. My hopes are growing but filled with great fear, for I know not when you'll be coming near. My dreams are to hold you till the mornings shining glare, but till then I'll often sit in Just a Stare.

Written and arranged by: Terry Lee McClain

"In Flow"

Life moves at a tasteful pace when the mind is never set in a thoughtless waste. Today starts off with a staring glance... Then thoughts consume the mind to break the trance. The direction is not yet clear for where to go... But apparently we must begin if only just to be in flow. We move about in a lazy manner hoping that nothingness will allow us to wave the victory banner. We seldom have any direct path to go... But we must continue on our plight as we go in flow. The troubles we face are basically the same... But the ones we can't endure, we only have ourselves to blame. If we love one another as we walk to and fro... Then lights of glory brighten our path as we continue along life's destiny constantly and smoothly in flow.

Written and arranged by: Terry Lee McClain

"IF"

If only I could see you, the warmth of your touch would carry me through. If the beauty of flowers and trees could express my love, you would know my passion for you comes from above. If once again life would grant me a wish, it would be to embrace you with a warm tender kiss. If I could feel your love as when the wind blows, then my heart would glitter with joy as when a diamond glows. If I could sleep with you once again through the night, my heart would be at peace with the comfort of holding you tight. If tomorrow brings me another day, my dream would be to walk with you far far away. If only you could know how much I love you so, then you would think of me everywhere you go.

Written and arranged by: Terry Lee McClain

"Happy Birthday, Son"

As the moon gives light with a subtle glow and the river runs with its powerful flow, so does the sun emit its dazzling rays. Therefore, I hope you see many more birthdays.

Written and arranged by: Terry Lee McClain

"Just To You"

Like a cold winter breeze you send chills down my spine and like a sun set over the ocean you stay on my mind. Like a warm summer wind by the sea you will always mean the world to me. And like sitting by the bay watching the current ripple away I think of you and wish you a Happy Valentine's Day.

Written and arranged by: Terry Lee McClain

"You Deserve"

You deserve happiness and so much more, you deserve a good long life, then the keys to heaven's door. You deserve all the joy that life can give in every way; so, on this special day, you deserve to have me say, I love you and I know that above all you deserve on earth, you deserve a Happy Birthday!!! So, Happy Birthday!!!

Written and arranged by: Terry Lee McClain

"Wait For Me"

My love for you is clearly plain to see, tha question is will you wait for me? When yellow flowers blossom to a bloom, my memories of you begin to consume. My every thought, my every dream, my every wish is to hold you. As sleep overshadows my sight to see, my thoughts through tha night are will you wait for me? As another day is once again at hand, my dreams are to walk with you along tha sea shore sand. As I press on through this ongoing day, my heart fills with passion that with me you will always stay. The worth of diamonds and pearls could never delight my joy; but to hold you would be better than a child receiving a new toy. The vision in my mind looks upon tha beautiful roaring sea and my heart sings with love of tha question of will you wait for me?

Written and arranged by: Terry Lee McClain

"I Will Never Lie"

My feelings for you reach far beyond the sky, because to you I will never lie. Time nor space can never keep us apart for you will always be a part of my heart. Even though my nights are spent alone, I know we will embrace again and all my troubles will be gone. My thoughts of you are all through the night, my dreams are constantly of holding you tight. Even now as I care so much for you, it makes me want to cry and to you I will never lie. I only hope to hold you again once before I die, for you mean the world to me and to you I will never lie. My days are spent for you in a distant stare and someday soon I know we will awake to the mornings shinning glare. When we are together again and I wipe a tear from my eye, our love will soar like the eagles fly and to you I will never lie.

Written and arranged by: Terry Lee McClain

"My feelings of You"

My every breath brings me closer to death and yet never can I fully explain my feelings of you, but you are my love, indeed it is true and no one else will ever do. Every day my soul sings with joy for the comfort of feeling the space you have left in my heart; the space that no one else will ever employ. The never ending pain you left me so dearly, keeps my mind, heart, and soul in darkness seemingly yearly. If I could vision a view of the passion I hold for you, it would be the vision of a setting sun: Far beyond the edges of a ever roaring sea, the sky is illuminated with orange fading light, the clouds are gathered in a scattered haze of gray, the sun falls down, and a shadow of darkness gently cloths the sky. Someday the darkness you have cast upon my lonely soul will be changed to an ever glowing light; but till then, I will only sleep with hopeful dreams of you each and every night. When my days and nights are again filled with blissful joy and my life begins brand new; my memories are ever of the caring love we shared and forever and always my feelings of you.

Written and arranged by: Terry Lee McClain

Terry Lee McClain

"A Bed of Roses"

I looked out through a window one summer day; yes, in a stare at what was out there and what was out there became the focus of my distant stare. I was looking across a field fully clothed with wheat. A gentle breeze swept casually over the top to give the buds a neat and unique sway. I began to see the beauty of the field as my thoughts became more intense and how lovely it looked through the wooden fence. There was also a bed of roses by the fence. They were yellow and open, wet with droplets of dew. The sun had burst its wonderful and glorious light upon them. And, oh how splendid did the roses look with the sun light upon them. The whole scene was truly beautiful and reminded me of someone I once knew. Then the true reason for my stare was all there in plain view, it was the roses and I was only thinking of you; it was as though I was looking directly at you. That is when I realized that it could only be a bed of roses such as this one that could display the beauty that comes close to reminding me of the beauty of the woman I see in you. And, oh what a beautiful bed of roses I saw that summer day.

Written and arranged by: Terry Lee McClain

"You Know All About It"

As I sit with my face clasped within my hands, like a dream I suddenly began to ponder. When take back stands at the door and money you have no more, when you can't find a job because you don't know Bob, and when your lights offer no day because you just couldn't pay. Jesus, I know you know all about it. When your son calls and says, hey daddy, how are you today? Can I have twenty dollars? He's excited, he's filled with joy, and you know it's somewhere fun he wants to go. His voice sounds different, even somewhat unique, and all you can say is son I'm sorry, I didn't get a pay check this week. Jesus, I know you know all about it. When frustrations cover you like the warmth of a blanket when it's cold and it seems to be no relief from the troubles of old, or perhaps the more left to unfold. Jesus, I know you know all about it. When it seems like the world offers you no future, no happiness, nor gain and the dark clouds above you stay open just to rain. Jesus, I know you know all about it. And, as I ponder my plight, I know every decision I make from now must be right. I'll get up again and stand as a man, because I know I must carry on with Gods plan. Jesus, I know you know all about it. But on that day in heaven when all the angles begin to play. Joy shall pass over me like a broom over a dusty floor, happiness shall whisper in my ear; go ahead, make plans for the new year, and peace shall release a powerful sigh saying, my child tonight inside you won't have to cry. Jesus, I know you know all about it. Yea, Jesus, Lord Jesus, I know you know all about it.

Written and arranged by: Terry Lee McClain

"New Born"

Precious as a new day at dawn, I know you are beautiful as a new born fawn. Here to cast a cascading blanket of shinning light to make others believe that hope in the word is still beaming bright. Here to laugh and play into the upcoming day. You will conquer the ups and downs of life and triumph in victory when you reach the top. I will always pray that at your quest for happiness you will never stop. Remember always that your blessings come only from above and the " Lord of All Understanding " delivered you here with His uncontested love.

Written and arranged by: Terry Lee McClain

These two poems were written to me from my son:

"Half Man Half Amazing"

You are the only man I know that's half man half amazing, It's like the rest of the cows were full and you were the only cow still grazing. It was like you wanted more in life so you kept on grazing, and that's exactly why you're half man half amazing. I tip my hat off to the man that graduated after two decades, at first you popped like a firecracker, and then you exploded like grenades. You Terry McClain, are history in the making and that's why I call you half man half amazing.

Written and arranged by: Philip Austin McClain

"The Meaning of L.O.V.E. to Me"

<u>Let</u> not your heart be troubled for your son understands, his daddy is also now his father and a relationship he demands. <u>Obstacles</u> we both will hurdle together in

life's journey of ups and downs, the past is gone let's finish strong for we both deserve crowns. <u>Visions </u>of us setting examples for others that forgiveness exist, and the ignorance of feeling hate towards your loved one is foolishness. <u>Embrace</u> this very defying moment that broken hearts were reconstructed, negativity is extinct we are no longer reluctant.

"Like Father, Like Son"
Love, Philip

Written and arranged by: Philip Austin McClain

Words of encouragement

"The Challenge"

Never let the other man see your troubles and defeats openly. Sleep with them thyself alone and rest, because today cometh and thou must shew thyself a man. The man was set in the earth to rule and no color was ordered. So, when you awake take thy spirit with thee whithersoever thou goest and the spirit that breaths within shall guide you. Keep your head up and carry the spirit, because it can see all things. We walk by faith, not by sight. So go forth today as a man and tomorrow you will gladly stand. Tomorrow is always your today, so as yesterday you stood as a man; proud, dignified, and ready to challenge the world. Bring that man before the world again and again and again, then one day the world will gladly accept the same happy man they saw yesterday and soon they will trouble you no more, because you shewed thyself a man. That's the key my friend, no matter the adversity, shew thyself a man; always, because " remember "... Your troubles slept with you last night and rested. Today they can only follow you as far as you will let them. Shew thyself a Man.

Written and arranged by: Terry Lee McClain

"No Fear"

When the time comes for the setting of our earthly sun, let no fear invade your mind, don't worry about what's left behind. There is no need for us to dread the unknown fate that lies ahead, we know that we were born to die, that can't be changed no matter how we try. One consoling thought can always be. Christ took the sting out of death for you and me. So we think of it as an open door, that we pass through to receive much more. We should have no fear of the unknown because of the love our Lord has shown. He promised us a home and we should believe it, but we must pass through deaths door to receive it.

Author, unknown

A quote from Mr. Quincy Jones to Mr. Michael Jackson (my favorite musical artist of all times) from the December 2007 edition of Ebony Magazine, as advice to Mr. Jackson: Let the song talk to you. If a song needs strings it will tell you. Get out of the way and leave room so that God can walk in. Jones agrees, "that was his motto". You've got to leave space for God to walk through the room. <u>It's not about us. The older I get, the more I see how little we all have to do with anything, really ".</u>

Spoken by: Mr. Quincy Jones
Acknowledged by me: Saturday 04.18.2009

My formula for peace within:

1. Life is a continuation of moments that must be approached with little or few mistakes as possible.
2. One must begin to change his/her continuation of moments by eradicating mistakes through belief in Jesus Christ. "There is no other way".
3. One must begin to accept that his/her continuation of moments have been altered from the natural course as is acceptable to society in order to become willing to restore value in his/her continuation of moments or life.

Formula: A = Acceptance, C = Change, B = Belief, P = Peace

Thus: " A " is accepting that your life has been thrown off its original course. " C " is realizing that a decision must be made by you alone that a " change " must occur in your life. " B " is belief in God, only through Jesus Christ that your life can be restored to a progressive state. And " P " is peace within one's self when the proceeding 3 letter combinations are applied to one's self or life.

As follows: $P = A + C / B$

P (peace within) = Acceptance + Change / Belief

Written and derived by: Terry Lee McClain

1. Nothing external to me can have any power over me... Walt Whitman
2. I shall allow no man to belittle my soul by making me hate him... Booker T. Washington
3. Every noble work is at first impossible... Thomas Carlyle
4. *When you get into a tight place and everything goes against you, till it seems as though you could not hold on a minute longer, never give up then, for that is just the place and time that the tide will turn... Harriet Beecher Stowe*
5. Can you walk on water? You have done no better than a straw. Can you soar in the air? You have done no better than a fly. Conquer your heart; then you may become somebody... Ansari of Heart
6. Fore, the kingdom of heaven is within you... Jesus Christ our Lord

Farewell and remember, I hunt.

Author, Terry Lee McClain (Monday 01.14.2013)

Continue to pray for me as I do for you and all others.

ACKNOWLEDGEMENTS

I WOULD LIKE TO thank Jesus Christ first and always for the ability and skills to write. My thanks goes out to my Moma (Sally), my daddy (the late Robbie); for without them this book would not be possible. Also, I would like to thank the numerous people that have been a part of my life for without each and every one of them this story could not have materialized. My six brothers, whom are all still living (blessed be the Lord) and all have a respectable degree of success; even to the degree of attorney at law (Timmy of Flordia) and Anthony of Lowell NC, Roydell of Asheville NC, Ronnie of Flordia, Rogers of Altavista Virginia, and Charles of Kings Mtn NC. To my aunts and uncles of Shelby NC; Annie Mae, Doris, Margret & Rick, Bobby, Woodrow, Bryant & family, cousins (Doran & Danny), and all other kin people that have helped to shape my life and this story. Thanks also to my aunts and uncles on my daddy's side of the family (especially Uncle Charles of Flordia) and the rest of the McClain clan of Kings Mtn NC and the surrounding areas. Also, a special thanks to the staff of the SARRPT program (a substance abuse program) at the VA hospital of Salisbury NC and my class mates, the staff members of ABCCM (a veterans restoration quarters program) of Asheville NC (Director Micheal and case manager Eddie) they were a very positive influence toward my well being. Also, to my Son (Philip of Charlotte NC, his daughter and my precious grand-daughter "Ariah" and her caring mother "Sheree"). Thanks to "Buck" & his family, James "Peter Rabbit", and Thomas. Ann and her family of Shelby NC, Jerome, Duriel, Crystal, Cassidy, Dennis Jr.(DJ), Denisha, James, Alberta, Shante, Robert, Daniel and his family, Issac and his wife Wyonia and family, Deborah, Jimmy Dean, Sylvia, Marggie, the late Albert Lewis, Judge Daughton, Herald & Patsy & family of Stanley NC, and all other friends and relatives (the late and the living).

DEDICATION

To Marvelous of whom I love dearly, and my mother Sally, and my only son Philip, my grand-daughter Ariah and her mother Sheree. You are my crew and I Love you. Also, to the young people of America and the world over without end.